DANCING CATS
AND
NEGLECTED MURDERESSES

EDWARD GOREY

WORKMAN PUBLISHING
NEW YORK

Library of Congress Cataloging in Publication Data

Gorey, Edward St. John.
Dancing cats and neglected murderesses.
Drawings originally prepared for Cat catalog and
D. Winn's Murderess ink. — cf. Publisher's catalog.
1. Cats — Caricatures and cartoons. 2. Murder —
Caricatures and cartoons. 3. American wit and humor,
Pictorial. I. Title.
NC1429.G536A4 1980 741.973 79-56533
ISBN 0-89480-082-5

Workman Publishing Company, Inc.
1 West 39 Street
New York, New York 10018

Manufactured in the United States of America

First printing March 1980
10 9 8 7 6 5 4 3 2 1

DANCING CATS

in which
cats are shown engaged,
for reasons known only to themselves,
in a wide variety of unlikely pursuits,
many of them being of a rather mysterious nature.

Butterfly cat drifting aimlessly
on a summer afternoon.

Cheerleading cat
with crepe paper chrysanthemums.

Cat supering in the third act
of *Il Combattimento di Asparago e Scallioni*.

Cat delivering a classical oration
in suitable surroundings.

Cat who has forgotten how to cast off
knitting a muffler.

Cat on a tightrope to celebrate
the opening of a falls.

Cat with pea and walnut shells
hoping to deceive.

Cats taking a barre in
all sorts of lumpy and subfusc garments
traditional for this endeavour.

Cat doing calligraphic flourishes
on a remote pond.

Cat making an entrance in a
drawing room comedy.

Cat in a vase playing Bach
on an unaccompanied flute.

Cat portraying the legendary
emperor Oshii Koto
in the Noh play *Neko no Pijama*.

Commedia dell' arte cat practicing
sleeve gestures.

Cat semaphoring *A Psalm of Life*
to the world in general.

Cat giving tarot card readings
of a dismal nature.

Spectral cat appearing
in the air
above a croquet wicket.

**Cat being nonchalant
at a fashionable skating rink.**

Famous cat burglar
waiting for a light
to be extinguished in a pantry.

Cat about to conduct
a hitherto unknown overture.

Another butterfly cat
caught by a sudden gust of wind.

Cat juggling impromptu
raisin cookies on the back porch.

Cat in a comic recitation
of a rustico-ethnic persuasion.

Cat wondering if the wires will hold
during not only the finale
but also the curtain calls.

NEGLECTED MURDERESSES

Angelica Transome

so disposed of her infant brother
that he was not found
until many years later (Nether Postlude, 1889).

Miss Elspeth Lipsleigh

eventually succeeded
in causing the death of Arthur Glumm
at Towage Regis, 1892.

Nurse J. Rosebeetle

tilted her employer out of a wheelchair
and over a cliff
at Sludgemouth in 1898.

Mrs. Fledaway

laced her husband's tea
with atropine in the spring of 1903
at the Locusts, near Puddingbasin, Mortshire.

Sarah Jane ("Batears") Olafsen

hacked to collops nineteen loggers
between March 1904 and November 1907
in and around Bindweed, Oregon.

Madame Galoche

in May 1911 added a tin of insecticide
to a potage purée Crécy aux perles
at the soup kitchen she operated for the indigent
of Berchem-Sainte-Agathe, Belgium.

Miss Emily Toastwater

smothered her father after evening prayers,
London S.W.7 (1916).

Mrs. Daisy Sallow

eviscerated her daughter-in-law with a No. 7 hook,
afterwards crocheting,
over the course of three evenings,
her shroud in a snowflake pattern (1921).

Natasha Batti-Loupstein

pulverized a paste necklace
and sprinkled it over a tray of canapés,
Villa Libellule, Nice, 1923.

Lady Violet Natheless

strangled the Hon. Opal Gentian at Gilravage Hall
on Midsummer's Eve, 1925.

Lettice Finding

shot Edgar Cutlet, whose mistress she was,
during the interval of a touring repertory company production
of *Rosmersholm*
in Manchester in 1934.

Miss Q.P. Urkheimer

brained her fiancé
after failing to pick up an easy spare
at Glover's Lanes, Poxville, Kansas, 1936.

Edward Gorey

is both author and illustrator
of more than thirty unusual
literary gems.
Fifteen of these were republished
in the best-selling
Amphigorey,
followed by a second collection,
Amphigorey Too.

In 1977
he designed the
Tony-award winning sets
for the Broadway show *Dracula*.